John XXIII
(a short biography)

• • •

KERRY WALTERS

Franciscan
MEDIA
Cincinnati, Ohio

Cover and book design by Mark Sullivan
Cover painting © Peter Wm. Gray, S.S., PH.D.
Original painting is hanging in the
Theological College of Catholic University of America

LIBRARY OF CONGRESS CATALOGING-IN-PUBLICATION DATA
Walters, Kerry S.
John XXIII : a short biography / Kerry Walters.
pages cm
Includes bibliographical references and index.
ISBN 978-1-61636-751-0 (alk. paper)
1. John XXIII, Pope, 1881-1963. 2. Popes—Biography. I. Title.
BX1378.2.W355 2013
282.092—dc23

2013037595

ISBN 978-1-61636-751-0

Published by Franciscan Media
28 W. Liberty St.
Cincinnati, OH 45202
www.FranciscanMedia.org

Printed in the United States of America.
Printed on acid-free paper.
14 15 16 17 18   5 4 3 2 1

For
Nora Clare,
My goddaughter

Contents

Introduction

Il Buono Papa

Angelo Giuseppe Roncalli, who became Pope John XXIII in 1958, was supposed to be a do-nothing pontiff, a transitional placeholder whose occupancy of Peter's throne would give curia power brokers some breathing space to think about who they wanted to succeed him. He was a month short of seventy-seven when he was elected, the oldest pope since Clement XII in 1730. Come what may, everyone in the conclave assumed his reign would be short.

Most curia officials also guessed he would be easily controllable. Although Roncalli was patriarch of Venice in the years preceding his election as pope, he didn't stand out as obvious papal material. He had been a good but not exceptional student and seminarian, and as a priest, he got off to a dubious start by hitching his wagon to a view of the Church frowned on by the hierarchy. In a day when most leaders of the Italian Church were recruited from old patrician families, it didn't help that Father Roncalli's unglamorous features testified to the peasant stock from which he came. He was broad faced, big eared, thick lipped, and prone to corpulency.

Never a curia insider, Roncalli was raised to the episcopate in middle age for reasons of protocol rather than perceived merit. As a Vatican diplomat in a backwater of Europe for nearly twenty years, he was grossly underappreciated. At a particularly humiliating moment, he was made to kneel before the papal throne for a solid hour and endure a chewing-out about something for which he was entirely blameless. His appointment as papal nuncio to France a year later wasn't much of a rehabilitation; the position needed filling quickly, and the pope's first choice had turned the job down.

During his years in France, many of Roncalli's colleagues in the diplomatic corps as well as several members of the curia saw him as an affable amateur. And when he became cardinal and patriarch of Venice at the end of 1952, Vatican watchers judged it the terminus of a rather undistinguished career.

The underestimation that followed Angelo Roncalli for much of his life is a startling example of how even the Church can sometimes mistake humility for mediocrity. Early on, the future pope had adopted as his own the maxim of St. Gregory of Nazianzen: *Non voluntas nostra sed voluntas Dei pax nostra*—"Not our own will but the will of God is our peace."[1] Throughout his long life he strove to live up to those words through obedience to God and the Church. For him, this meant always choosing less rather than more and seeking the lowest rather than the highest place, resolutions that many of his peers misread as weakness, naïveté, or worse.

But God writes straight with crooked lines. The same spiritual gifts that misled cardinals in the 1958 conclave to see Roncalli as a safe choice also enabled him to revitalize the Church during his brief pontificate in ways none of his contemporaries anticipated. During his four and a half years as pope, John XXIII breathed fresh life into the Church by convening the Second Vatican Council. He was exactly the person to do it, exemplifying as he did a spirit of openness to Christians of all denominations.

Although a loyal son of the Church, he welcomed a respectful dialogue between the contemporary secular world and Christianity, and he courageously reached out to world leaders to urge peace and sanity during one of the Cold War's most precarious moments. Despite the pomp and circumstance of his office, he remained intensely and lovably human, sometimes ending his addresses with a homey request for parents to go home and give their kids a kiss from Pope John. By the time he died in 1963, no one thought of him as a do-nothing pope. Instead, he was affectionately called *Il Buono Papa,* "the Good Pope," by nearly everyone. And so he was.

chapter one

Apprenticeship in Holiness

"Let your will be mine, and let my will ever respond to yours, in perfect accordance."[2]

—Angelo Roncalli, *Journal of a Soul*

Later in life, Angelo Roncalli couldn't recall a time when he didn't want to be a priest. But his sharecropper father, Giovanni, had doubts. The Roncalli family had worked the land near the Lombardy village of Sotto di Monti ("under the mountain") since the fifteenth century. That's all they knew how to do. Giovanni worried that Angelo would make a poor priest. It was above his station in life.

The fourth of thirteen children, the future pope was born on November 25, 1881, in a two-story farmhouse that was home to an extended family of thirty-two people, not to mention several farm animals sheltered on the ground floor. Life was hard. Half of the kale, milk, veal, and silk produced each year by the Roncallis went to their landlord. John XXIII remembered that the family ate polenta instead of bread and that shoes and clothing were handed down from one sibling to the next. But despite the poverty, his childhood was a happy one.

Don Francesco Rebuzzini, the parish priest who baptized Angelo, recognized the boy's promise, even if Giovanni didn't, and began tutoring him in Italian (residents of Sotto di Monti spoke a local dialect) and Latin. By the time he was eleven, Angelo was ready for junior seminary in the town of Bergamo, just eight miles away. In 1895, he entered senior seminary and began keeping a journal at the suggestion of his spiritual director. In it, the adolescent Roncalli recorded his struggles to pray mindfully, to apply himself diligently to his studies, and in all matters to conform his will to God's. He was critical, sometimes exaggeratedly so, of what he considered his failings: vanity, self-love, laziness, and even occasional "excessive mirth," although thankfully he also noted that it was, after all, "always better to be merry than to be melancholy."[3] Roncalli would continue his journaling for the rest of his life, eventually filling nearly forty notebooks.

Most of the entries from his seminary days record the kinds of predictable resolutions one would expect from an earnest young man preparing for ordination. At one point, he drew up a calendar of daily, weekly, monthly, and annual spiritual disciplines that would have exhausted him had he kept to it. Such is the zeal of youth. But one journal entry, written in September 1898, stands out. In it, Angelo recorded the death of his mentor and friend Don Rebuzzini. The old cleric, who Angelo credited with "set[ting] me on the way to the priesthood," was stricken in the church sacristy while preparing for Mass. Angelo discovered his body, its "mouth open and red with blood," looking "like a statue of the dead Jesus, taken down from the Cross."[4]

The loss of the priest who was like a second father "was the greatest sorrow I have ever suffered in my whole life,"[5] and a distraught Angelo referred to himself as an orphan several times in his journal. It was his first encounter with the harsh mystery of death. In the long years ahead, he would mourn the passing of many: parents, siblings, friends.

But as we'll see, only two other deaths hit him as hard as Rebuzzini's, the man whom he ever afterward thought of as "the saintly guardian of my childhood and vocation."[6] As a memento, the stricken youth took Rebuzzini's well-thumbed *Imitatio Christi*. As he lay dying in the apostolic palace sixty-five years later, Pope John XXIII asked that passages from that very copy be read to him.

Angelo traveled to Rome in early 1901 to complete his studies at the Pontifical Roman Seminary, the Apollinare. But by November he had left the life of a student for a year of mandatory military service that he caustically referred to as his "Babylonian captivity." Despite his distaste for the experience, he seems not to have suffered too badly. He was stationed close to home in Bergamo, was eventually promoted to sergeant, and achieved high marks on the rifle range. But he complained in his diary that the army was "a running fountain of pollution, enough to submerge whole cities,"[7] and thanked God that he had remained unsullied. "I passed through the mire and by his grace I was kept unpolluted.... Jesus, I thank you, I love you."[8]

After serving his time in the army—an experience that would be repeated under quite different circumstances thirteen years later—Roncalli returned to the Apollinare for another year and a half. In mid-July 1904 he obtained his doctorate in theology and less than a month later, after a retreat in which he divided his time between fervently praying and anxiously practicing Mass, he was ordained a priest on the feast of St. Lawrence. The following day he said his first Mass at the tomb of St. Peter and had a brief audience with Pope Pius X, during which he received the pontiff's blessing. Then it was on to Sotto di Monte, to celebrate Mass in his hometown.

While celebrating for the first time in St. Peter's, Don Roncalli felt overcome by love of God and awe at his new status as a priest. He felt that the marble and bronze statues of popes in the huge basilica gazed on him "with a new expression, as if to give me courage and great confidence."[9] Filled with deep gratitude, he repeated the words of Peter (John 21:17): "Lord...you know that I love you." This first prayer of the new priest Don Roncalli would also be the final one of Pope John XXIII.

Christ and the Social Order

"Jesus stooped to wash the feet of the twelve poor fishermen. This is true democracy, of which we ecclesiastics should be most eloquent examples for all to see."[10]

—Angelo Roncalli, *Journal of a Soul*

It's unlikely that Pius X followed the career of the newly ordained priest he blessed in 1904. But if he had, he would have been disappointed. During the next decade, Don Roncalli embraced a view of the Church's social responsibility that the pontiff despised, and he remained loyal to it for the rest of his life.

By the year of Angelo Roncalli's birth, relations between the kingdom of Italy and the Vatican had soured to the point where Catholics were forbidden to participate in politics. Catholic Action, a movement aiming at the promotion of social justice, was formed as a nonpolitical alternative. Inspired by Leo XIII's 1891 encyclical *Rerum Novarum,* Catholic Action defended workers' rights, supported labor unions, and encouraged low-interest mortgages so that peasant sharecroppers could purchase their own land. Angelo's father was a grateful recipient of one of those loans, and Bergamo, where Angelo was educated, was a major center of Catholic Action activity. So both family experience and schooling instilled in him the conviction that Christ charged his followers to be concerned with spiritual well-being *and* social justice.

But Pius X couldn't have disagreed more. Primarily concerned with battling what he took to be intellectual, cultural, artistic, and political threats to the Church—all rather indiscriminately lumped together as "modernism"—he disliked democracy, distrusted social reformers, and resolved to root out or at least muzzle clergy who thought otherwise. In 1904 he abolished *Opera dei Congressi,* an umbrella lay movement inspired by Catholic Action. Two years later, he came perilously close to condemning democracy in his encyclical *Vehementer Nos.*

In 1907, his *Pascendi Dominici Gregis,* an encyclical that condemned modernist "heresies" and threatened excommunication to anyone who disagreed, ushered in an era of what can only be described as ecclesial spying and repression. So-called "councils of vigilance" were established throughout Europe to ferret out suspected modernists among the clergy. One alarmed bishop called the period the "white terror."

One of the priests caught in Pius's dragnet was Giacomo Radini Tedeschi, a nobly born priest who had been active in *Opera dei Congressi.* After dissolving the organization, the pope kicked

Radini Tedeschi upstairs by making him bishop of Bergamo. The promotion removed the progressive-minded priest from Rome, exiled him to a provincial diocese, and effectively silenced him—or so Pius hoped. It didn't quite work out that way.

Roncalli and Radini Tedeschi had met in 1899, and when the new bishop took up his duties in Bergamo he invited the young priest, exactly half his age, to serve as his secretary. It was the beginning of an extremely fruitful period for Roncalli, who soon became known as "the bishop's shadow."[11]

Radini Tedeschi replaced Don Rebuzzini as the father figure in Roncalli's life. The two frequently traveled together out of Italy, making several trips to the shrine at Lourdes and one to the Holy Land. It was during his period of service to Radini Tedeschi that Roncalli, who had a special devotion to the sixteenth-century saint Charles Borromeo, began editing the Borromeo archives in Milan, a task that would eventually fill thirty-nine volumes and be completed only in 1957, the year before Roncalli became pope.

Most importantly, Roncalli, in collaboration with his bishop, quietly continued the work frowned on by the pope. Now teaching in the Bergamo seminary, Roncalli gave lectures that cautiously recommended textual and historical analysis of Scripture, a method that Pius dismissed as "modernist." For his part, Radini Tedeschi continued to advocate for workers' rights, doing so as much under the radar as possible. But sometimes his efforts to keep a low profile were less than successful.

In 1909, after he contributed to a fund that supported striking textile factory workers, conservatives publicly condemned the act as an endorsement of socialism. Radini Tedeschi was unruffled by the attack, but his bulldog Roncalli went on the offensive. In a newspaper essay that appeared in late 1909, he wrote that the Church was obliged to intervene when people were treated unjustly. Catholic clergy should emulate the Good Samaritan. In tending the wounds injustice and poverty inflicted on the underprivileged, they were heeding "Christ's preference" for "the disinherited, the weak, and the oppressed."[12]

Roncalli's defense of Radini Tedeschi didn't go unnoticed by the curia, as he discovered many years later. Flipping through his large personnel file after he was elected pope, he saw that someone had noted in it years earlier that he was "suspected of Modernism." Outraged, he scrawled a reply: "I, John XXIII, declare that I was never a Modernist!"[13]

Roncalli's years with Radini Tedeschi, whom he ever after affectionately referred to as "my bishop," solidified his commitment to a vision of the Church open and receptive to the needs of the world. When Radini Tedeschi died in August 1914, two days after Pius X, Roncalli was heartbroken for the second time in his life. But with the election of Pope Benedict XV, who in his first encyclical signaled a break with his predecessor by declaring, *Christianus mihi nomen, Catholicus cognomen* ("Christian is my name, and Catholic my family name"), Roncalli sensed a new wind blowing through the Church. He regretted only that his bishop hadn't lived to see it.

By this time, World War I had begun. Roncalli was mobilized in 1915 and put to work as a medical orderly in a Bergamo hospital treating wounded soldiers. During the war years, he tenderly ministered to thousands of men, admiring their bravery and self-sacrifice but growing to hate war as the greatest evil that befalls humans. Personal worry added to his spiritual distress over the carnage of war: Two of his brothers fought with the Italian army, and one of them went missing and was feared dead before turning up in a POW camp. When Roncalli was finally demobilized in December 1918, he was weary to the bone with the charnel house the world had become. He wanted a ministry that celebrated life.

Apostolic Delegate

"The Apostolic Delegate is a bishop for all and intends to honor the Gospel, which does not admit national monopolies, is not fossilized, and looks to the future."[14]

—Angelo Roncalli

Roncalli found the life-affirming ministry he was looking for when he was appointed warden of a hostel for lay students in Bergamo. He loved the job. It gave him the opportunity to teach and offer spiritual counseling, a combination that brought him great satisfaction. After the horror of war, he felt rejuvenated by the young people.

Much as he loved the post, he held it for less than three years before Benedict XV tagged him for a leadership role in the Society for the Propagation of the Faith. Founded in 1822, the society's task was to collect donations for the Church's missionary activities. Roncalli's job was to consolidate fundraising efforts. He had qualms about taking on the assignment, protesting that he was lazy and, of all things, a slow writer. But he excelled in this new ministry, more than doubling the society's collection in his first two years.

Two events occurred in 1922 that signaled a sea change in Roncalli's life: Pope Benedict died, and Mussolini and his fascist party took power in Italy. The new pope, Pius XI, entered into talks with Mussolini that culminated, seven years later, in the Lateran Treaty's recognition of the Vatican as a sovereign and independent power. In the early 1920s, Pius wanted no cleric rocking the unstable negotiations boat.

Unfortunately for Roncalli, that is precisely what he did. In the autumn of 1923 he delivered a sermon that warned against trusting Mussolini's overture to the Church, claiming it was insincere window dressing. This broadside was bad enough. But to make matters worse, Roncalli, who was also teaching patristics to seminarians in Rome, shocked his superiors—and students—by suggesting that mixed marriages between Catholics and non-Catholics might, in some circumstances, be justifiable.

These two missteps were apparently enough to set off alarms in the Vatican. Within months, Roncalli suffered the same fate that had befallen his bishop twenty years earlier: he was kicked upstairs and exiled to a backwater. Pius named him apostolic visitor (later changed to apostolic delegate) to Bulgaria and made him an archbishop on the pretext that otherwise Bulgarian bishops wouldn't respect his authority. By spring 1925, Archbishop Roncalli was in Sofia, Bulgaria's capital.

Roncalli spent the next nine years in a nation beset with political turmoil—the year before he arrived, more than 200 politicians, including the prime minister, had been assassinated—and with a total of only 45,000 Roman Catholics. The country's Muslim majority was largely indifferent to the Latin Church, while its Orthodox population was suspicious and often hostile.

As the first Vatican envoy to Bulgaria in six centuries, Roncalli knew he faced two tasks. Above all, he needed to pastor the tiny Roman Catholic community scattered throughout the nation. He also needed to improve relations between the Vatican and the Bulgarian Orthodox Church. To fulfill the first, he spent his initial months in Bulgaria touring the countryside with a Byzantine rite priest acting as interpreter. The two traveled by car and train when they could and by horse when the terrain became rough and mountainous, visiting rural Catholics who often lived in poverty similar to what Roncalli had known as a boy in Sotto di Monte. Along the way, he listened, preached, comforted, and blessed. He also ordered that prayers at Mass be said in Bulgarian.

Rapprochement with the Orthodox Church was more difficult. He met with the Orthodox patriarch, prayed in Orthodox monasteries, and tried his best to create an ecumenical climate of trust. But Orthodox wariness only began to give way a little after a series of deadly earthquakes hit Bulgaria in the spring of 1928. Roncalli immediately set out to the stricken areas to minister to the homeless and injured. He slept in tents with them, comforted them in their despair, and made a nuisance of himself to his Vatican superiors until they sent him relief funds to open refugee centers that became known as the "Pope's soup kitchens."

For the most part, though, Roncalli's years in Bulgaria were frustrating ones. The Vatican seemed not to care much about him or his mission (except for the occasion when he was recalled and made to kneel while the pope berated him), and despite his best efforts, the Orthodox hierarchy remained aloof. But Roncalli grew to love the Bulgarian people. When he was transferred to Turkey and Greece in late 1934, his final sermon extended an invitation to any Bulgarian, regardless of his or her religion or social status, to always feel free to visit him. "You will find the candle lighted in my window…. Two fraternal arms will welcome you and the warm heart of a friend will make it a feast-day."[15]

In many ways, Roncalli's new assignment was more frustrating. There was even less of a Roman Catholic presence in Turkey and Greece than in Bulgaria. As part of his campaign to westernize Turkey, President Kemal Atatürk began replacing religious schools with public ones, suppressing religious publications, and forbidding the wearing of religious habits. In Greece, the government refused to recognize Roncalli's diplomatic credentials and became even more hostile to him after Italy invaded Abyssinia in 1935.

As in Bulgaria, Roncalli focused on pastoring Catholics and conciliating non-Catholic critics. He wore a suit and bowler hat in Istanbul, learned enough Turkish to speak it at Mass, and ordered both the Gospel and litany read in Turkish. In Greece, he prayed at Orthodox monasteries and churches and visited Mount Athos, later joking about how hard it was for him to stay on horseback while traversing its narrow paths.

Balancing on horseback was a good metaphor for his ministry in Turkey and Greece, which required him to pastor his flock without riling local prejudices. But his exposure to non-Catholic religious traditions during these years convinced him that dialogue with them was absolutely necessary. As a pastor who also happened to be a diplomat, he unfailingly stressed that no Church, his or any other, held a monopoly on God. Jesus "died to proclaim universal brotherhood," he declared from a Turkish pulpit. "The central point of his teaching is charity—that is, the love which binds all men to him as the elder brother, and binds us all with him to the Father."[16]

A Terrible *Periculum*

"War is desired by men, deliberately, in defiance of the most sacred laws. That is what makes it so evil."[17]

—Angelo Roncalli, *Journal of a Soul*

Roncalli deplored a Christian chauvinism that rejected some children of God as spiritually lost simply because of the creed they professed. Similarly, he despised nationalism for its adversarial division of the world's people into superior "us" and inferior "them." "The world is poisoned with morbid nationalism built up on the basis of race and blood, in contradiction to the Gospel."[18]

These words were written in late 1940, fourteen months into World War II. Remaining as apostolic delegate to Turkey and Greece throughout most of the war, Roncalli devoted himself to relief work. He pulled what diplomatic strings he could to get food to starving civilians caught in the crossfire of battle and get exit visas to Jews fleeing the Nazis. He badgered the Vatican to exert pressure on both the Allied and Axis powers to treat prisoners of war humanely.

As one of "God's consuls," he believed it his sacred obligation to advocate for all victims of war without privileging one side or the other. His position gave him, he said, "the holy freedom to present himself to the conqueror in the name of a spiritual authority, and in the name of the interests of the conquered people."[19]

The September 1939 blitzkrieg against Poland that ignited the war created the conflict's first wave of refugees. Roncalli quickly organized a committee in Istanbul to collect supplies for them. After it became clear that Greece was an Axis target, he received orders from the Vatican to divert most of his attention from neutral and out-of-danger Turkey and toward imperiled Greece. Roncalli visited the nation on three different occasions before Italy invaded it in October 1940. The Greeks managed to resist Mussolini's armies, but fell the next year to the Wehrmacht. The British navy immediately imposed a blockade, cutting off food and medical supplies to the occupied Greeks.

By the time the blockade was lifted a year later, nearly half a million had starved to death. During the terrible months of hunger, Roncalli did his best to get grain into Greece, and persuaded Pope Pius XII, elected only months before war broke out, to set aside Vatican funds for famine relief. The following year he unsuccessfully begged the German commander of occupied Athens to spare the lives of captured partisans. At the beginning of the war, Roncalli had written that "war is a terrible *periculum,* danger. For the Christian who believes in Jesus and his Gospel it is an iniquity and a contradiction. 'Deliver us, O Lord, from famine and war.'"[20] The occupation of Greece was a nightmarish verification of his words.

In addition to his efforts to help the Greeks, Roncalli also became involved in two other humanitarian tasks. No doubt recalling the capture and imprisonment of one of his brothers in World War I, he worked with the Red Cross to trace prisoners of war in order to get relief packages to them and word of their condition to their families. His patient persistence paid off; representatives of all the warring nations except the Soviet Union cooperated with him. The Soviet position was that any Russian soldier who allowed himself to be captured was a de facto traitor.

The fate of the Jews in Nazi-occupied Europe had become clear early on in the war, and Roncalli was sickened by it. "Poor children of Israel," he wrote in early 1943. "Daily I hear their groans around me. They are relatives and fellow-countrymen of Jesus."[21] In 1943 and 1944, his overriding focus was getting as many Jews to safety as possible. He began by badgering the Vatican into officially requesting that Britain lift the restrictions preventing refugee Jews from entering Palestine. When the British government refused, Roncalli turned elsewhere. He found a willing accomplice in, of all people, Franz von Papen, the German ambassador to Turkey.

Together, they arranged to supply Jewish refugees in Istanbul with money and documents.

Roncalli also intervened to urge Bulgaria's King Boris, whom he knew from his time in Sofia, to resist persecution of that nation's Jews. When a detailed plan of how the Nazis intended to orchestrate the "final solution" in Bulgaria was sent to his Istanbul office, he was horrified. He immediately sent a cable to Boris, who soon afterward began issuing transit visas to Palestine for Slovakian Jews. The king was poisoned the following year, probably by the Nazis and almost certainly because of his resistance.

In his efforts to smuggle Jews out of Nazi-occupied lands, Roncalli couldn't bring himself to write fake baptismal certificates, although he didn't condemn others who did. But he personally made sure that thousands of transit visas issued by the Palestine Jewish Agency, with which he closely worked, got to refugees. Von Papen later testified that Roncalli was responsible for saving the lives of nearly twenty-five thousand Jews.

Roncalli might have saved thousands more but for the Vatican's silence. In early 1943, the Palestine Jewish Agency asked him to lobby the pope for three favors: to ask neutral countries to accept Jewish refugees whose upkeep would be underwritten by American Jews, to inform the German government that the Palestine Jewish

Agency had five thousand transit visas it would gladly give to German Jews, and to make a public statement to the faithful urging them to help Jews. Roncalli took the message to Vatican officials, who quickly declined to get involved.

Historians have debated the moral propriety of the Vatican's silence in the face of Hitler's slaughter of Europe's Jews. Some maintain that a public condemnation of the Holocaust would have hamstrung the Church's behind-the-scenes efforts to aid refugees; others see the silence as inexcusable anti-Semitism. What's undeniable is that Roncalli worked tirelessly on behalf of the "poor children of Israel." After the war, Isaac Herzog, chief rabbi of Jerusalem, applauded him as "a man who really loves the People of the Book, and through him thousands of Jews were rescued."[22]

Nuncio and Patriarch

"Without a touch of holy madness, the Church cannot survive."[23]

—Angelo Roncalli, while French Nuncio

In December 1944, a sixty-three-year-old Roncalli was informed that Pius XII had named him nuncio to France, the most prestigious post in the Vatican Foreign Service. He wasn't the first choice, a fact which one curial official rather rudely let him know. But the post badly needed filling, and Pius was willing to go with Roncalli. For his part, Roncalli took his second-place status in stride. When horses won't run, he quipped, donkeys must trot.

As nuncio, Roncalli was the Vatican's ambassador to the newly-liberated French government. He had no pastoral duties, and in fact could visit dioceses or parishes only at the invitation of bishops. But during his nine years in France he managed to travel to all but two of the eighty-seven dioceses, including ones in French North Africa. He relished the visits, and tirelessly endured thousands of miles by car and train to make them. His humility and humor easily won him the love of French Catholics. Once, at the end of a sermon, he smilingly acknowledged to the congregants that his French wasn't very good. But it made little difference, he went on to tell them, because he probably hadn't said much worth attending to anyway.

Shortly after he arrived in France, Roncalli was faced with a diplomatic storm. War-hero and president Charles de Gaulle accused twenty-five bishops of collaborating with the Vichy government during the Nazi occupation and demanded their removal by the Vatican. The Vatican, in turn, insisted that because the Vichy government had been legitimate, the bishops were legally justified in not resisting it. Roncalli's gentle touch managed to defuse a standoff that risked blowing up postwar relations between France and the Vatican. Eventually seven of the offending prelates were retired.

More difficult for Roncalli was Pius XII's crackdown on French worker priests and French theologians. The worker priest movement had been launched during the war years; the idea was for incognito priests to accompany workers deported to German labor camps and factories in order to tend to them spiritually while working alongside them. After the war, many worker priests continued this unconventional style of ministry and became outspoken advocates for workers' rights. Pius, who believed they'd been corrupted by communist ideology, outlawed the movement.

At around the same time, the pope issued *Humani Generis*, basically an update of Pius X's repressive *Pascendi Dominici Gregis*'s assault on "modernism." In the new encyclical, Pius XII roundly condemned historical analysis of Scripture, a method Protestant scholars had used for a century. Although not calling them out by name, the encyclical implicitly rebuked and silenced several prominent scriptural scholars, especially the French Dominicans Marie-Dominique Chenu and Yves-Marie Congar, both of whom Roncalli knew.

Roncalli's disagreement with Pius's assault on French worker priests and scholars became clear after he was elected pope. As John XXIII, he applauded priests who took the material welfare of their flock seriously, shrugging off the predictably ensuing accusations that he was soft on communism. In his opening address to the Second Vatican Council, he welcomed the historicist approach to reading Scripture. The "deposit of faith, or truths, which are contained in our time-honored teaching is one thing," he said, "the manner in which these truths are set forth is something else."[24]

John XXIII also made sure that the silenced theologians were rehabilitated, and many of them went on to act as *periti*, or theological advisors to the council. But as nuncio to France under Pius XII, he kept silent. It was his duty as the pope's representative to support Vatican decisions, or at least not to publicly contest them. So at the time, he limited himself to the wry observation that an occasional touch of holy madness is healthy for the Church.

In the closing days of 1952, the patriarch of Venice fell ill and died. Roncalli, now seventy-one and feeling his years, was named successor and raised to the cardinalate. The new appointment wonderfully revitalized him, and he relished the five years he held it. Venice offered him the opportunity to be a pastor in his own country after nearly thirty years of diplomatic exile.

Although the "gem of the Adriatic," Venice was a city with a huge unemployment problem. There was little the new patriarch could materially do about the poverty except to give generously from his own purse and support politicians, even socialists, who advocated for the poor. But he could and did make sure that his flock knew he loved them and cared about their well-being.

He was soon tirelessly zipping to every quarter of the city in the *vaporettos,* or water buses. He announced that his goal was to visit every parish and then, in the spirit of open collegiality, to hold a diocesan synod. He accomplished both of those goals, and during the three-day synod that took place in late 1957, he told the assembled priests that the Church's two greatest internal dangers were an authoritarianism that "stifles life" and a paternalism "that keeps people immature."[25] It was an extraordinary observation for a prince of the Church to make.

Two years earlier, Roncalli had delivered three lectures on Christian unity that were equally extraordinary. In them, he not only called for a spirit of cooperation between Catholics, Orthodox, and Protestants—a move in itself frowned upon by many in the Church—but he also suggested that there was enough blame for the divisions in the eleventh and sixteenth centuries to go around. The Catholic Church had to acknowledge and repent of its fair share if the rupture was ever to be healed.

And then, in October 1958, something everyone had expected for several years happened: Pius XII, who had been ill for some time, died. Roncalli had disagreed with the pope many times, but remained silently obedient to the man who was Peter's successor. As a cardinal, he was eligible to vote in the conclave that would elect Pius's successor. Three days after the pope's death, he headed to Rome, expecting to return to his beloved Venice shortly.

Vocabor Johannes

"'My little children love one another.' Love one another
because this is the great commandment of our Lord."[26]

—John XXIII, Address to the Conclave

Angelo Roncalli was elected pope on October 28, 1958. It took
three days and eleven ballots for the conclave to agree that the aged
patriarch of Venice would be a good stopgap pontiff who would do
nothing and then conveniently die.

During most of the final decade of Pius XII's reign, ill health had
forced him to hand over more and more authority to the curia,
the papal court responsible for administering the Vatican's various
departments. Upon his death, leading members of the curia, reluc-
tant to give up their power, preferred a compliant successor who
would maintain the status quo. They mistakenly thought they'd
found their man in Roncalli. As they quickly discovered, John
believed the task of Church leaders was "to cultivate a flourishing
garden of life" rather than to be "museum keepers."[27]

The first indication that the new pope was a cultivator instead
of a museum keeper occurred immediately after his election. In

response to the traditional question *Quomondo vis vocari?* ("How do you wish to be called?"), Roncalli replied, "*Vocabor Johannes,*" ("I wish to be called John"), explaining that it was the name of his father and of the two men "closest to Christ the Lord," John the Baptist and John the Beloved. Then he reminded the cardinals of Christ's great commandment to love. The radical inclusivity of Christ's love, symbolized by his outstretched arms on the cross, would be the hallmark of John's pontificate. And love, as the curia soon discovered, is the most powerful force in the world.

Five days later, even before he was installed, John raised the idea of an ecumenical council, the first in ninety years and only the twenty-first in the Church's entire history. But unlike the last one in 1870, John wanted this council to be about renewing the Church rather than circling the wagons against the modern world. *Aggiornamento*—prosaically translated as "updating" or "renewal" but suggesting an exciting period of rejuvenation—became the proposed council's catchword.

Curial conservatives were shocked by this unanticipated move on the part of what was supposed to be a do-nothing pope. Their leader was Cardinal Alfredo Ottaviani, formidable head of the Congregation of the Holy Office whose personal motto, *Semper idem* or "Always the same," perfectly expressed his view of Church reform. Although ultimately outvoted at every turn by the Second

Vatican Council, he would fight *aggiornamento* tooth and nail. Increasingly dismayed by the fresh breeze blowing through the Church, he once expressed the hope that he would die before the council ended its work so that he could meet his maker while still a "good Catholic."

Elected pope just short of his seventy-eighth birthday, John was well aware that his time was short. So he moved council preparations along with dispatch, but not so swiftly as to bewilder curial officials more accustomed to a slower pace or totally alienate Ottaviani and his supporters. At the same time, John took his pastoral responsibilities as the bishop of Rome seriously. Realizing that his age made it impossible to visit all of the city's parishes, he opted instead for a diocesan synod, similar to the one he had held in Venice. When it met in 1960, John saw it as a rehearsal for the worldwide ecumenical council he was planning.

Another indication that John felt the urgency of time was the fact that he issued no fewer than eight encyclicals during the 1,680 days he was pope. Five of them appeared in the first year and a half of his pontificate. The second and third were conventional enough, focusing on the duties of priests and devotion to the rosary. The first and fourth, concentrating on Christian unity and indigenous churches, gestured at the spirit of *aggiornamento* John wanted the council to embrace.

The fifth encyclical, *Mater et Magistra,* released in May 1960, did more than gesture. It testified to John's long fidelity to the principles of economic and social justice promulgated in Leo XIII's 1893 *Rerum Novarum,* defended by his beloved mentor Giacomo Radini Tedeschi, and practiced by the worker priest experiment of the 1940s. A privileging of the world's hungry and oppressed, John argued, was mandated by Christ. Salvation remained the Lord's first gift; "but He [also] showed His concern for the material welfare of His people when, seeing the hungry crowd of His followers," he ordered them fed. Fidelity to "Christ's command to *give*" obliged the Church to stand firmly with the "hungry crowd."[28]

Standing firmly meant doing something about injustices like low wages and deplorable working conditions. As a recipe for healing social wounds, John applauded Leo's principle of subsidiarity: Redress should begin at the local level and move upward only if local efforts prove unsuccessful. He took the principle to its logical conclusion by arguing that it could also, if necessary, justify political or centralized supervision of the economy. John was no opponent of private property, but he decried an unjust distribution of wealth that privileged the few over the many. "The divine Master frequently extends to the rich the insistent invitation to convert their material goods into spiritual ones by conferring them on the poor."[29]

One of the more touching features of the encyclical was John's worried discussion of the "depressed state of agriculture," to which he devoted a full twenty-six paragraphs. In writing about the need for credit banks, fair taxation, price protection, and social insurance for farmers, he was clearly pulling on his experience as the son of a poor sharecropper.

Finally, John ended *Mater et Magistra* with a guide for "rebuilding a social order based on truth, justice, and love."[30] Such rebuilding required hard work and active participation in the world on the part of the faithful. "Let no man therefore imagine that a life of activity in the world is incompatible with spiritual perfection."[31] Although he didn't say so, John XXIII was living proof of the assertion's truth.

Conservatives in Europe and the United States raised red flags before the ink had scarcely dried on John's encyclical. The *National Review* captured their mood in August 1960 by quipping, "Going the rounds in Catholic conservative circles: '*Mater si, Magistra no.*'"[32] But in this fifth encyclical, John had discovered his voice. He proclaimed to the world that the Church's business was the spiritual *and* material well-being of *all* human beings, regardless of their religion, and that the Vatican would gladly work with governments, social agencies, and non-Catholics to that end. If the Roman synod had been a rehearsal for a global conciliar gathering, *Mater et Magistra* was a preview of the council's agenda.

seven

Prelude to a New Pentecost

"What is needed is that certain and immutable doctrine,
to which the faithful owe obedience, be studied afresh and
reformulated in contemporary terms."[33]

—John XXIII, *Gaudet Mater Ecclesia*

The first session of Pope John's council convened on October 11,
1962. Three years of rigorous planning had preceded it. In 1959,
questionnaires were sent to 2,822 bishops, abbots, and Catholic
educators around the world inviting them to suggest topics for the
council's consideration. The response rate, nearly 77 percent, was a
good barometer of the excitement that the prospect of an ecumenical council stirred up.

A preparatory committee spent months carefully examining the
feedback. It created ten commissions charged with drafting pro-
posals on specific issues such as liturgy or theology, which would
then be submitted to the council when it met. Each commission
was manned by sixteen bishops appointed by curial leaders like
Cardinal Ottaviani. Not surprisingly, most of them were opponents

of *aggiornamento* who deplored the pope's *pruritus innovationum* or "itch for innovation."

Thankfully, within days of convening, council members overwhelmingly voted to reject the members of each of the commissions and replace them with candidates of their own choosing. A furious Ottaviani condemned the move as a scandalous act of public insubordination. But council delegates—and, one suspects, John—believed the ground was now cleared for genuine progress. As one of the theological advisors to the council remarked afterwards, "An apple tree produces apples, a cherry tree cherries."[34] The council wanted a different kind of fruit than the curia was offering.

In the spirit of openness, Pope John made it clear that he wanted the council's proceedings to be public; eventually some 1,200 reporters from around the world covered the event. He also insisted that representatives from other Christian traditions be invited as observers and treated respectfully. His intent from the start was for this to be a genuinely ecumenical council. Shortly before it convened, John greeted the forty non-Catholic observers in a papal audience. Contrary to custom, he insisted that his throne not be elevated. He would greet his guests as a fellow Christian, not a prince of the Church.

At the council's opening ceremony, nearly 3,000 people, including 85 cardinals, 2,131 bishops, dozens of abbots and superior generals from religious orders for men (but not, alas, leaders of women's orders), and assorted *periti* crammed into St. Peter's Basilica. After a three-hour ceremony, John delivered a homily he had written with great care. It was in Latin, as all the proceedings of the council would be. (Translators were available for reporters, non-Catholic observers, and more than a few prelates unable to follow the Church's lingua franca.) It was arguably the most significant sermon of his life.

John made several key points that would guide the council's spirit and work. He emphasized that the gathering was a cause for thanksgiving, celebration, and joy. "Prophets of doom" such as Ottaviani (although the pope didn't mention him by name) who insisted that the world was going to hell in a hand basket were mistaken. On the contrary, "present indications are that the human family is on the threshold of a new era,"[35] and it was the Church's obligation and privilege to respond with faith and optimism. This required thinking about how to present ancient and revered doctrine in ways that would speak to the new era.

The purpose of the council, then, was to celebrate the doctrines of faith and present them "in contemporary terms." In fulfilling this mission, the Council would both renew the Church internally and promote ecumenical reconciliation between the different Christian traditions, bringing closer the "unity for which Christ prayed on behalf of His Church."[36]

In keeping with his rejection of nay-saying and his embrace of dialogue with the world, John repudiated the Church's historical mode of "condemn[ing] with the utmost severity" doctrines and theologies she found objectionable. Now, he asserted, "Christ's Bride prefers the balm of mercy to the arm of severity. She believes that present needs are best served by explaining more fully the purport of her doctrines, rather than by publishing condemnations."[37]

And with that, John bowed out of the council's proceedings lest his presence inhibit the free flow of discussion. He observed via closed-circuit television and regular written reports, but kept his distance until the final meeting sixty days later. During those two months, in addition to the election of new bishop-commissioners, the Council accomplished the essential task of setting up an agenda for what needed to be tackled in future sessions. Cardinal Giovanni Battista Montini, the future Pope Paul VI, drew it up. He estimated that the council would need to meet two more times.

As things turned out, a total of four sessions were required, the final one convening in 1965. But the Council's most important achievement in its first session was its overwhelmingly approved decision (1,922 to 11) to allow Mass to be said in the vernacular instead of Latin. With that historic vote, the Church opened her doors and invited the world in.

On the council's final day, John congratulated the assembly for what it had achieved. Sensing that some members felt disappointment at not having accomplished more this first time around, he reassured them that the inaugural session "was like the slow and majestic prelude to a great masterpiece."[38] Council members had come from widely scattered points on the globe, and it had taken time for them "to understand one another's hearts." Now that they were brothers, future sessions would be even more fruitful. "Then, doubtless, will dawn that new Pentecost which is the object of our yearning." In the meantime, he told them to go home and continue the "hidden, silent work" of prayer.[39]

It was a bittersweet parting for John, because he knew that he would never witness the new Pentecost he joyfully predicted. Just days before the council convened, the stomach cancer that would kill him less than a year later was discovered. He was a marked man, and he knew it. Now, he told intimates, the only thing he had to offer the council was his suffering.

chapter eight

Peace on Earth

"The world will never be the dwelling place of peace, till peace has found a home in the heart of each and every man, till every man preserves in himself the order ordained by God to be preserved."[40]

—John XXIII, *Pacem in Terris* (1963)

Less than a week into the council, the world came chillingly close to nuclear holocaust. Aerial photos revealed that Soviet missile sites were being built in Cuba. President Kennedy threw a blockade around the island, Premier Khrushchev threatened to break it, and for an entire week it seemed likely that the long-standing Cold War between the globe's two nuclear superpowers was about to become a devastatingly hot one.

As the crisis grew increasingly perilous, Kennedy solicited John's help. In his weekly radio address, aired on October 24, the pope obliged by calling for restraint on the part of both leaders, and followed it up with a private note to Khrushchev. His public plea for peace gave the Soviet premier the excuse he was looking for to back away from the nuclear standoff. The missiles were pulled out of Cuba, and the world breathed a sigh of relief.

The following spring, John's peacemaking efforts to defuse the crisis were recognized by the Balzan Prize, an international humanitarian award. His willingness to reach out to Khrushchev, the leader of an avowed anti-Christian state, had not only helped end the immediate threat of nuclear war, but it also inaugurated a relaxation of the mutual distrust between the Vatican and the Kremlin, leading in December 1962 to the release of Josef Slipyi, head of the Ukrainian Catholic Church, who had been imprisoned in a Soviet gulag since 1945. Slipyi, an *in pectore* or secretly named cardinal, was the inspiration for novelist Morris West's 1963 bestselling *The Shoes of the Fisherman.*

In the wake of the Cuban Missile Crisis, a desperately ill John set to work on what he knew would be his final encyclical. The document, *Pacem in Terris,* was released on Holy Thursday, 1963. John chose that date because it commemorates Jesus's commandment to his disciples to love one another.

The encyclical, the full title of which is "On Establishing Universal Peace in Truth, Justice, Love, and Liberty," is a brief for taking God's love for creation as the standard in social, economic, and political affairs. God's natural order, John argued, is structured by love and reason. The human order, if it is ever to achieve harmony, must conform to it. "Peace on earth…can never be established, never guaranteed, except by the diligent observance of the divinely established order."[41]

The terrible game of nuclear brinksmanship played by the U.S. and the Soviet Union in Cuba was the immediate inspiration for *Pacem in Terris*. But John had been thinking and praying about peace and justice for years. World War I unforgettably impressed on him the evil of warfare. Experiences in violence-torn Bulgaria and Greece, not to mention the horror of the Holocaust, only confirmed his conviction. His impoverished boyhood, as well as the tutelage of both Catholic Action and Bishop Radini Tedeschi, showed him that economic and social injustices breed the anger that leads to bloodshed.

In his final message as pope, he wanted to draw upon both theology and experience to offer a way out of the spiral of violence. To signal his wish to speak to the entire world's people and not just Catholics or Christians, he broke precedent by addressing his encyclical to "all men of good will."

John's argument in *Pacem in Terris* revolved around the notion of natural rights, a novel approach in encyclical literature. Humans, created in God's likeness, possess a natural dignity, and this in turn bestows upon them certain rights which a well-ordered society must respect. Humans have a right to life and a reasonable standard of living, to freely search for and express truth, to worship God according to their conscience, to marry or not, to assemble, to immigrate, and to take part in political movements. These rights are universal and immutable. When human society honors them, it becomes "primarily [the] spiritual reality" God intends it to be, by which John meant a reflection of the divine love and reason that permeates the natural order.[42]

What threatens both natural rights and social harmony is the hatred bred by economic inequality, xenophobia, racism, and the subjugation of minorities and women. (John celebrated the fact that "women are [finally] gaining an increasing awareness of their natural dignity" and "demanding both in domestic and in public life the rights and duties which belong to them as human persons."[43])

On a global scale, these factors raised walls of distrust and antagonism between nations that led to the stockpiling of weapons of mass destruction. The consequence is that people live "in the grip of constant fear,"[44] dreading at every moment that a nuclear "storm may break upon them with horrific violence," and this chronic anxiety in turn only serves to ratchet up the distrust and hatred that encouraged the stockpiling in the first place. But this insane state of affairs is contrary to the love and reason that structure the universe. "Hence justice, right reason, and the recognition of man's dignity cry out insistently for a cessation to the arms race."[45]

John called on all humans to recognize their kinship with one another and to work for the restoration of justice and peace on earth. He charged Christians in particular with the task of reconciliation. "Everyone who has joined the ranks of Christ," John wrote, "must be a glowing point of light in the world, a nucleus of love, a leaven of the whole mass."[46] It was a heavy responsibility, but one he had willingly shouldered throughout his sixty years as deacon, priest, bishop, patriarch, and pope. Now, at the end of his life, it was time to pass it on to others.

Ite, Missa Est

"Lord, you know that I love you."[47]

—John XXIII's Dying Words

Three days after *Pacem in Terris* was released, Pope John celebrated Easter Mass in St. Peter's. Although he managed to make it through the long service, he was in nearly unbearable pain the whole time. Observers noted that he looked considerably thinner, was pale, and seemed bone weary.

In fact, the pope would be dead in six weeks from the carcinoma diagnosed the previous September. Cancer was the Roncalli family curse. Two of John's thirteen siblings died of it before him, and three more after. Several of them, including his beloved sister Ancilla, had the same stomach cancer that afflicted him. After Father Francesco Rebuzzini's and Bishop Radini Tedeschi's deaths, Ancilla's 1953 passing was the one that most devastated John. Shortly after her funeral, a confidante heard him sadly mutter, *Guai a noi se fosse tutta un illusione* ("Woe to us if it's all an illusion").

Roncalli was already more than seventy when Ancilla died, and had just been named patriarch of Venice. Her passing hit him as hard as it did because it reminded him of the sad irony that even though he was beginning an exciting new ministry, he was nearing his own end. In his *Journal*, he confessed that being poised "on the threshold of eternity" made him "tremble at the approach of my last hour."[48]

But in the very next sentence he affirmed his trust in God and resolved to "only look one day ahead"[49] instead of dwelling on his mortality. Such point-counterpoint reflections on death became regular features of his *Journal* in the years that followed. They were never far from his mind after he became pope.

By the late spring of 1963, he was literally and not just metaphorically on eternity's threshold. His cancer, inexorable as it was cruel, was entering its final stages. In early May, he began vomiting blood and was in such constant pain—John told his secretary that he felt like St. Lawrence roasting on the grid iron—that he needed sedatives to snatch even a few hours of restless sleep.

The pope celebrated his last Mass in the middle of the month, after which his strength utterly deserted him. On May 28, his condition had deteriorated so rapidly that the Vatican newspaper *L'Osservatore Romano* finally announced he was suffering from cancer. Up to that point, official announcements had attributed the pope's obvious weight loss to "gastric distress."

The beginning of the end came two days later when peritonitis set in after the pope's cancer ruptured an intestine. Upon hearing from his secretary that he hadn't long to live, John simply said, "Help me die as a bishop or a pope would."[50] Over the next seventy-two hours, as the infection spread and his organs began to shut down, the pope said his farewells to gathered family, staff, and curial officials.

At one point, gazing at a crucifix on the wall of his room, he pointed to it and declared it the "secret" of his ministry. "Look at it, see it as I see it," he said to the assembled members of the pontifical household. "Those open arms have been the programme of my pontificate: they say that Christ died for all, for all. No one is excluded from his love, from his forgiveness."[51]

John was too modest. From the beginning of his ordained life, not just during his pontificate, he had served his Lord by opening his own arms to embrace the world in love, patience, compassion, and tolerance. The papal culmination of that love, bequeathed to "all men of good will," was *Mater et Magistra, Pacem in Terris,* and the great ecumenical council he called but wouldn't see to its conclusion.

John's open-armed love also yearned for unity rather than discord among Christians who, despite being children of the same God, had split in the eleventh and again in the sixteenth century. The ecumenical dream he infused into the Vatican Council remained with him to the end. In his last days, he continually whispered, *Ut unum sint,* "That they may be one." It was the prayer spoken by Jesus after the Last Supper. ·

Toward the very end, John asked to hear passages from the *Imitatio Christi* that had once belonged to his beloved Father Rebuzzini and which he had carried around with him for sixty-five years. Before he lost consciousness, he said firmly, "Lord, you know that I love you!" They were the same words young Father Roncalli had uttered shortly after his ordination.

In the evening of June 3, as the pope lay dying, a Mass before a great crowd in St. Peter's Square was held to help ease his final journey to God. Just as the traditional *Ite, Missa Est* ended the Mass, John XXIII, *Il Buono Papa,* breathed his last.

Conclusion

"From the saints I must take the substance, not the accidents, of their virtues."[52]

—Angelo Roncalli, *Journal of a Soul*

For half a century now, Vatican watchers have been intrigued by what they call the "Roncalli mystery": how a man so apparently ordinary was chosen by God to breathe new life into the Church.

And rejuvenate the Church Pope John certainly did. Led by his vision, the Vatican Council reframed the way Catholics think about religious freedom, the spiritual significance of the laity, and the relationship of the Church to secular power and culture, non-Catholic Christians, and peoples of other faiths. It made the liturgy more accessible to millions of Catholics and non-Catholics alike.

And in embracing the loving openness of Christ's outstretched arms that John urged upon it, the council went a long way toward ending the self-enclosed monarchical triumphalism the Church had defensively adopted since the Reformation. After Good Pope John, the Church was more pentecostal in spirit and more pastoral in approach. After him and because of him, the Church experienced a new springtime.

How, indeed, could the son of a peasant sharecropper accomplish all this?

The Roncalli mystery dissolves once we recognize that saints aren't one-size-fits-all superheroes. All of us are capable of becoming saints, but only if our sainthood is authentically our own rather than slavishly copied from someone we admire. Every Christian best serves God in the way that fits his or her temperament, talents, and shortcomings.

The greatness of St. John XXIII consisted in recognizing his particular charism—a devout willingness to be humble and little and obedient in the service of the Lord—and dedicating it to the greater glory of God. This embrace of who he was empowered him to open his heart and mind to the world without prejudgment and to love it in all its diversity. It was precisely this compassionate humility that earned him a reputation for mediocrity among his less discerning peers before he became pope and fueled the Roncalli mystery afterward.

Many of us take an entire lifetime to learn that we're called to find our own way to sainthood rather than unimaginatively mimic someone else's. But young Angelo Roncalli discovered this truth before he was even ordained a deacon. As a seminarian, he too had tried to please God by mechanically imitating the lives of saints he admired, much as an amateur painter might try to copy a

Rembrandt brushstroke for brushstroke. "I used to call to mind the image of some saint whom I had set myself to imitate down to the smallest particular."[53] By 1903, bitter experience had taught him the foolishness of this approach.

Then it dawned on him that what was important about the saints was their spirit, not the day-to-day details of their lives, and with this came a new and fruitful resolution:

> I must not be the dry, bloodless reproduction of a model, however perfect. God desires us to follow the examples of the saints by absorbing the vital sap of their virtues and turning it into our own life-blood, adapting it to our own individual capacities and particular circumstances.[54]

This is the key to the Roncalli mystery. It's what made Pope John's ordinariness saintly. It's also a good rule of thumb for the rest of us who wish to open our arms wide to embrace God and the world.

Notes

1. Ernesto Balducci, *John: The Transitional Pope,* trans. Dorothy White (New York: McGraw-Hill, 1965), 44.

2. John XXIII, *Journal of a Soul: The Autobiography of Pope John XXIII,* trans. Dorothy White (New York: Signet, 1965), 74.

3. John XXIII, *Journal of a Soul,* 119.

4. John XXIII, *Journal of a Soul,* 110.

5. John XXIII, *Journal of a Soul,* 110.

6. Peter Hebblethwaite, *John XXIII: Pope of the Century* (London: Continuum, 1995), 13.

7. John XXIII, *Journal of a Soul,* 152.

8. John XXIII, *Journal of a Soul,*167.

9. John XXIII, *Journal of a Soul,* 228.

10. John XXIII, *Journal of a Soul,* 156.

11. Alden Hatch, *A Man Named John* (New York: Image, 1965), 50.

12. Hebblethwaite, 34.

13. Greg Tobin, *The Good Pope: John XXIII and Vatican II* (New York: HarperOne, 2012), 53.

14. Quoted in Hebblethwaite, 74.

15. Tobin, *The Good Pope*, 61.

16. Jeanne Kun, ed., *My Heart Speaks: Wisdom from Pope John XXIII* (Ijamsville, Md.: The Word Among Us, 2000), 14.

17. John XXIII, *Journal of a Soul,* 295–296.

18. John XXIII, *Journal of a Soul,* 309.

19. Hebblethwaite, 89.

20. Hebblethwaite, 81.

21. Thomas Cahill, *Pope John XXIII* (New York: Penguin, 2002), 135.

22. Lawrence Elliott, *I Will Be Called John: A Biography of Pope John XXIII* (New York: E.P. Dutton, 1973), 164.

23. Elliot, *I Will Be Called John,* 199.

24. John XXIII, *Gaudet Mater Ecclesia,* in *The Encyclicals and Other Messages of John XXIII* (Washington, DC: TPS, 1964), 430.

25. Hebblethwaite, *John XXIII,* 130.

26. Hatch, 143.

27. Tobin, *The Good Pope*, 93.

28. John XXIII, *Mater et Magistra,* 1.

29. *Mater et Magistra,* 2.

30. *Mater et Magistra,* title of Part 4.

31. *Mater et Magistra,* 4.

32. Tobin, *The Good Pope,* 156.

33. *Gaudet Mater Ecclesia,* in *Encyclicals,* 430.

34. Hebblethwaite, *John XXIII,* 227.

35. *Gaudet Mater Ecclesia,* in *Encyclicals,* 427.

36. *Gaudet Mater Ecclesia,* in *Encyclicals,* 432.

37. *Gaudet Mater Ecclesia,* in *Encyclicals,* 432.

38. John XXIII, "Toward a New Pentecost," in *The Encyclicals and Other Messages of John XXIII* (Washington, DC: TPS Press, 1964), 241.

39. John XXIII, "Toward a New Pentecost," 444, 442.

40. *Pacem in Terris,* 5.

41. *Pacem in Terris,* 1.

42. *Pacem in Terris,* 1.

43. *Pacem in Terris,* 1.

44. *Pacem in Terris,* 3.

45. *Pacem in Terris,* 3.

46. *Pacem in Terris,* 5.

47. Hebblethwaite, *John XXIII,* 258.

48. John XXIII, *Journal of a Soul,* 337.

49. John XXIII, *Journal of a Soul,* 337.

50. Tobin, *The Good Pope,* 224.

51. Hebblethwaite, *John XXIII,* 256.

52. John XXIII, *Journal of a Soul,* 172.

53. John XXIII, *Journal of a Soul,* 172.
54. John XXIII, *Journal of a Soul,* 172.

Bibliography

Balducci, Ernesto. *John: The Transitional Pope*, trans. Dorothy White (New York: McGraw-Hill, 1965), 44.

Cahill, Thomas. *Pope John XXIII* (New York: Viking, 2002).

Elliott, Lawrence. *I Will Be Called John: A Biography of Pope John XXIII* (New York: E.P. Dutton, 1973).

Feldman, Christian. *Pope John XXIII: A Spiritual Biography* (New York: Crossroad, 2000).

Flannery, Austin, ed. *Vatican Council II: Constitutions, Decrees, Declarations*. Revised edition (Northport, N.Y.: Costello, 1996).

Hatch, Alden. *A Man Named John: The Life of Pope John XXIII* (New York: Image, 1965).

Hebblethwaite, Peter. *John XXIII: Pope of the Century* (London: Continuum, 1995).

John XIII. *An Invitation to Hope*, trans. John Gregory Clancy (New York: Simon and Schuster, 1967).

———. *The Encyclicals and other Messages of John XXIII* (Washington, DC: TPS, 1964).

———— *Journal of a Soul: The Autobiography of Pope John XXIII,* trans. Dorothy White (New York: Signet, 1965).

————. *Letters to His Family, 1901–1962,* trans. Dorothy White (New York: McGraw-Hill, 1970).

————. *Mission to France: Memoirs of a Nuncio, 1944–1953,* trans. Dorothy White (New York: McGraw-Hill, 1966).

Kun, Jean, ed., *My Heart Speaks: Wisdom of John XXIII* (Ijamsville, Md.: The Word Among Us, 2000).

Maalouf, Jean, ed. *Pope John XXIII: Essential Writings* (Maryknoll, N.Y.: Orbis, 2008).

McBride, Alfred. *A Retreat with Pope John XXIII: Opening the Windows to Wisdom* (Cincinnati: St. Anthony Messenger Press, 1996).

Tobin, Greg. *The Good Pope: John XXIII and Vatican II* (New York: HarperOne, 2012).

Treece, Patricia. *Meet John XXIII: Joyful Pope and Father to All* (Cincinnati: Servant, 2008).

About the Author

Kerry Walters is a professor of philosophy and peace and justice studies at Gettysburg College in Pennsylvania. He is a prolific author whose recent books include *Giving Up god to Find God: Breaking Free of Idolatry; The Art of Dying and Living;* and *John XXIII: A Short Biography.*